MAIASAURA

AND OTHER DUCK-BILLED PLANT-EATERS

Prehistoric World

MAIASAURA

AND OTHER DUCK-BILLED PLANT-EATERS

VIRGINIA SCHOMP

BENCHMARK BOOKS
MARSHALL CAVENDISH
NEW YORK

DINOSAURS LIVED MILLIONS OF YEARS AGO. EVERYTHING WE KNOW ABOUT THEM—HOW THEY LOOKED, WALKED, ATE, FOUGHT, MATED, AND RAISED THEIR YOUNG—COMES FROM EDUCATED GUESSES BY THE SCIENTISTS WHO DISCOVER AND STUDY FOSSILS. THE INFORMATION IN THIS BOOK IS BASED ON WHAT MOST SCIENTISTS BELIEVE RIGHT NOW. TOMORROW OR NEXT WEEK OR NEXT YEAR, NEW DISCOVERIES COULD LEAD TO NEW IDEAS. SO KEEP YOUR EYES AND EARS OPEN FOR NEWS FLASHES FROM THE PREHISTORIC WORLD!

Benchmark Books
Marshall Cavendish
99 White Plains Road
Tarrytown, New York 10591-9001
www.marshallcavendish.com

Library of Congress Cataloging-in-Publication Data

Schomp, Virginia.
Maiasaura and other duck-billed plant-eaters/ Virginia Schomp.
v. cm. — (Prehistoric world)
Includes bibliographical references and index.
Contents: The "good mother" dinosaur — Time line: the age of dinosaurs — Maiasaura's world — On the march — The last dinosaurs.
ISBN 0-7614-1545-9
1. Maiasaura—Juvenile literature. 2. Hadrosauridae—Juvenile literature. [1. Maiasaura. 2. Dinosaurs.] I. Title. II. Series: Schomp, Virginia. Prehistoric world.

QE862.O65S425 2004
567.914—dc21

2003002009

Front cover: *Maiasaura* Back cover: *Corythosaurus* Page 2: *Lambeosaurus*

Photo credits:

Cover illustration: The Natural History Museum, London / Orbis

The illustrations and photographs in this book are used by permission and through the courtesy of: *Marshall Cavendish Corporation:* 2, 10, 11, 12-13, 16, 17, 18, 19, 23, 24, back cover. *The Natural History Museum, London:* 8, 22; John Sibbick, 21; Orbis, 9, 20. *PhotoResearchers, Inc.:* © John Kaprielian, 25.

Map and Dinosaur Family Tree by Robert Romagnoli

Printed in China

1 3 5 6 4 2

For Melissa Martin

Contents

THE "GOOD MOTHER" DINOSAUR

A female *Maiasaura* peers into her nest. She is waiting for her eggs to hatch. At last she hears a tap-tap inside a shell. Crack! A small wet head appears. Then one tiny foot, then another. Finally the whole baby emerges. Soon its brothers and sisters hatch, too. Now the nest is filled with chirping, squirming, hungry babies. Back and forth the mother goes, again and again, bringing food. This good mother will care for her babies until they are strong enough to leave the nest and take their place in the dinosaur world.

When scientists discovered evidence of a dinosaur that fed and protected its young, they named it Maiasaura, *from a Greek word meaning "good mother."*

SHANTUNGOSAURUS
(shan-tun-go-SORE-us)
When: Late Cretaceous, 83–73 million years ago
Where: China
- One of the largest duck-billed dinosaurs
- Heavier than an African elephant

Duckbills like this big-bellied Shantungosaurus *probably spent most of their time feeding.*

Maiasaura belonged to a group of plant-eating dinosaurs called hadrosaurs. Near the end of the Age of Dinosaurs, the hadrosaurs were the most common land animals on earth. They had bulky bodies and long tails. Their broad flat beaks looked something like a duck's beak, or bill, so these dinosaurs are often called duckbills. On page 26, you can see how *Maiasaura* and the other duck-billed dinosaurs fit into the dinosaur family tree.

A QUESTION OF CRESTS

There were two different groups of duck-billed dinosaurs. One group had hollow bony crests on the top of the head. These bizarre-looking ornaments came in many shapes and sizes. They looked like helmets, hatchets, and even a unicorn's horn.

The other group of duckbills had small solid head crests or no crest at all. These "flat-headed" hadrosaurs included *Maiasaura*.

LAMBEOSAURUS
(LAM-bee-oh-sore-us)
When: Late Cretaceous, 76–72 million years ago
Where: Mexico, Montana, and Alberta, Canada

- **Long flexible neck for grazing over wide areas**
- **Tough leathery skin**

Lambeosaurus *crests were shaped like rounded helmets or double spikes. Hadrosaurs may have made loud hooting or trumpeting sounds by blowing air through their crests.*

PROSAUROLOPHUS
(PROH-sore-oh-loh-fus)
When: Late Cretaceous, 80–75 million years ago
Where: Montana and Alberta, Canada
- Low solid crest in front of eyes
- About twice as tall as a man

Flat-headed duckbills like Prosaurolophus *may have made calling sounds through inflatable air sacs in their nostrils.*

A CLOSE-UP LOOK

It is easy to tell that *Maiasaura* was a duck-billed dinosaur. Its long face was broad at the front, with a wide ducklike beak. Farther back in its jaws were hundreds of strong teeth.

A full-grown *Maiasaura* measured up to thirty-seven feet long—longer than two cars. A third of the dinosaur's length was its stiff heavy tail. Its back legs were long and sturdy, while its front legs were shorter and weaker. *Maiasaura* could walk on all fours or stand on just its back legs. It stood up and ran to escape from the fierce meat-eating dinosaurs that shared its world.

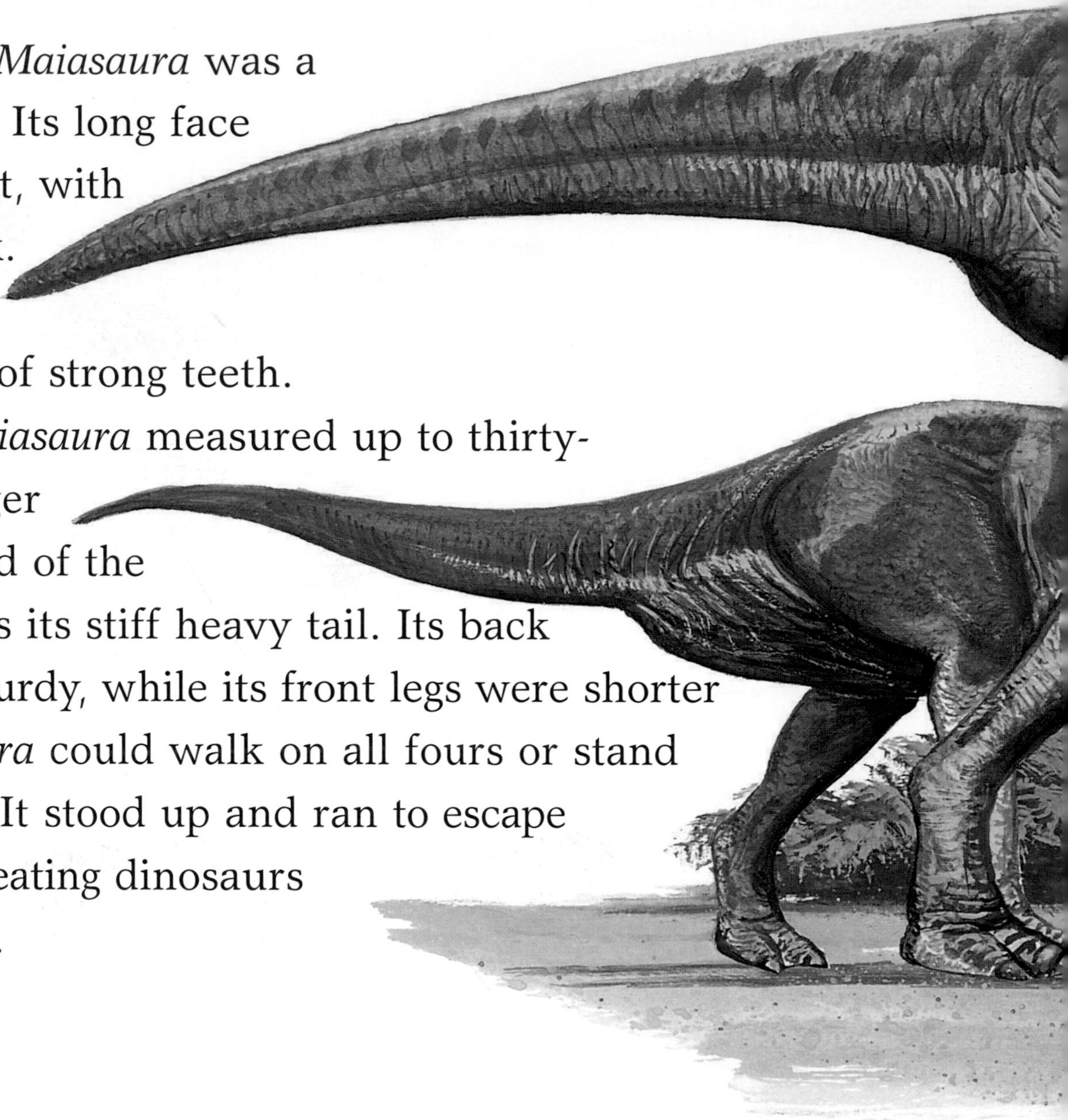

A young Maiasaura *walks beside its mother. No one knows what color dinosaurs were, but* Maiasaura*'s tough hide was probably colored to help it blend into the background so predators would have a harder time seeing it.*

MAIASAURA'S WORLD

Dinosaurs lived from about 230 million to 65 million years ago. In all that long time, the earth saw many changes. The continents moved. Oceans rose and fell. Mountains and volcanoes formed. By the end of the Age of Dinosaurs, the map of the world was beginning to look like it does today. But if we could travel back to those times, we would still find many surprises.

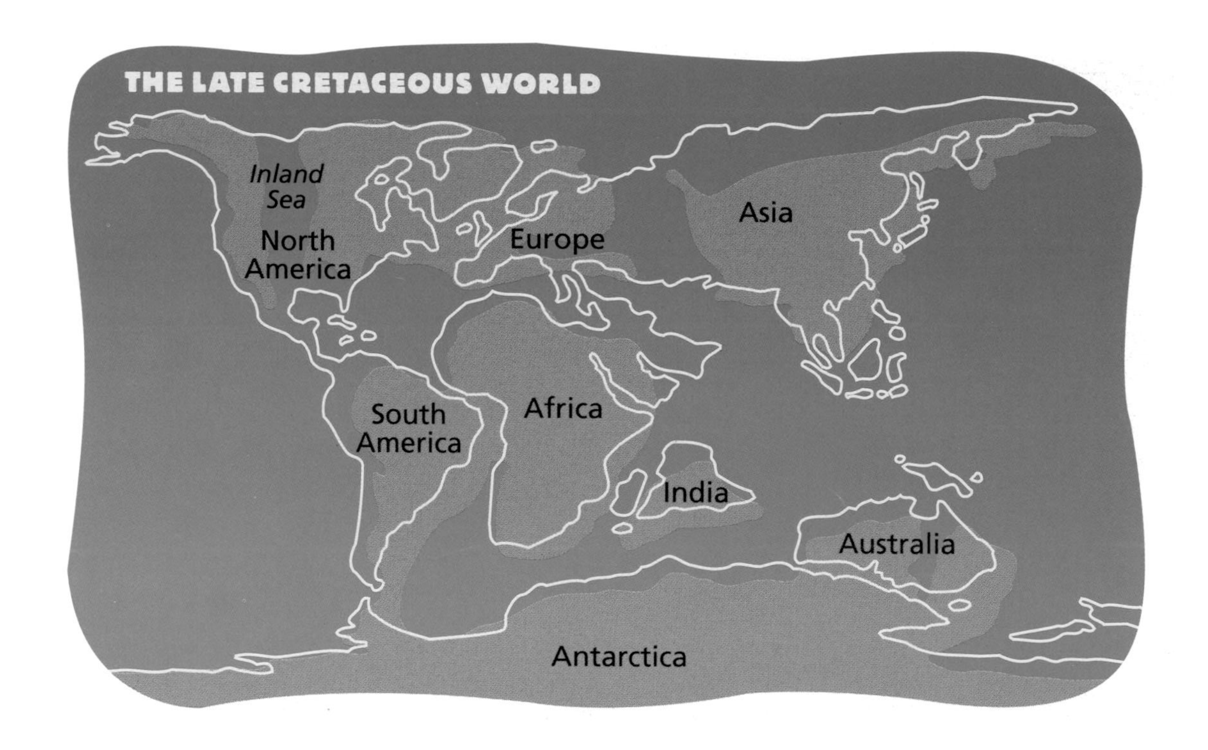

The earth's lands are always in motion. The yellow outlines on the map show the shape of the modern continents; the green shading shows their position around 73 million years ago, in the days of Maiasaura.

The Age of Dinosaurs

Dinosaurs walked the earth during the Mesozoic era, also known as the Age of Dinosaurs. The Mesozoic era lasted from about 250 million to 65 million years ago. It is divided into three periods: the Triassic, Jurassic, and Cretaceous.

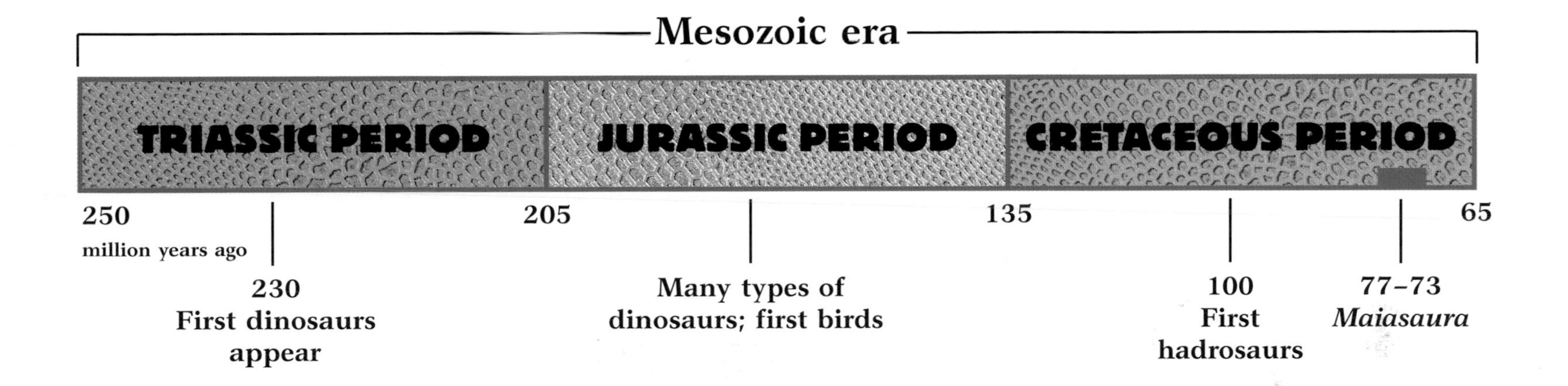

A LAND OF PLENTY

Our time machine takes us back 73 million years, to the Late Cretaceous period. A third of North America is underwater. A huge inland sea stretches from the top to the bottom of the continent, separating west from east. The western island is the home of *Maiasaura.*

It is a warm and wet home. Ferns, low leafy plants, flowering trees, and evergreen forests stretch as far as the eye can see. All this vegetation makes a never-ending feast for *Maiasaura.* Many other plant-eating dinosaurs share the riches of the land. There are different kinds of duckbills, as well as three-horned *Einiosaurus,* a cousin of *Triceratops*. Massive meat-eating *Albertosaurus* and small but deadly *Troodon* menace the plant-eaters and their babies.

BRACHYLOPHOSAURUS
(brahk-ee-LOH-fuh-sore-us)
When: Late Cretaceous, 75 million years ago
Where: Montana and Alberta, Canada
- Small solid crest above nostrils
- As long as a fire engine

Brachylophosaurus *was one of several kinds of duck-billed dinosaurs that lived in North America alongside* Maiasaura.

ANATOTITAN
(ah-nah-toe-TIE-tan)
When: Late Cretaceous, 70–65 million years ago
Where: Montana and South Dakota
- Name means "giant duck"
- Unusually long, flat skull

Duckbills got their name from their toothless beaks, but unlike ducks, the dinosaurs had strong teeth in their cheeks for grinding up tough plants.

There are other kinds of animals, too. Small furry mammals scurry underfoot. Flying pterosaurs rule the skies. The waters swarm with crocodiles, giant turtles, and long-necked reptiles with needle-sharp teeth.

ON THE MARCH

Let's travel across North America with *Maiasaura*. The plains and forests echo with the hooting and honking of huge hadrosaur herds. *Maiasaura* and the other duckbills live in herds for protection from predators. Each herd has hundreds or thousands of pairs of watchful eyes. When a duckbill spots a dangerous meat-eater, it sounds a warning. Even the hungriest predator will think twice before charging into a crowd of these big stamping, trampling animals.

CORYTHOSAURUS
(koh-RITH-oh-sore-us)
When: Late Cretaceous, 75–70 million years ago
Where: Montana and Alberta, Canada
- **Helmet-shaped hollow head crest**
- **May have made hooting sounds through breathing tubes in crest**

Corythosaurus*'s odd-looking head crest may have provided a clue to the dinosaur's age and whether or not it was male or female. The crests grew as the dinosaurs got older, and males had larger crests than females.*

Hadrosaurus *and the other duckbills did not have sharp claws or armor like some other dinosaurs. They lived in herds for safety, and they may have run on two legs to escape from predators.*

Hypacrosaurus *fed mainly on low-growing leaves, twigs, and branches.*

The herd we are following is making its yearly journey to its nesting grounds. Along the way, the duckbills chomp on leaves, twigs, berries, pine needles, pinecones—just about any plant they can find. A *Maiasaura*'s wide toothless beak can scoop, snip, and tear off mouthfuls of food. Hundreds of cheek teeth grind even the toughest plants to a pulp. The duckbill's teeth get worn down from all that chewing, but new ones constantly grow in to replace them.

IN THE NURSERY

After weeks of travel, the *Maiasaura* herd reaches a high plain far from the sea. Now the females get busy. Using their feet and snouts, they pile up mounds of soft soil and scoop out nests. The center of each nest is six feet wide—roomy enough for fifteen or twenty eggs. After the mothers lay their eggs, they may pile soft leaves and ferns on top. The plants will rot, giving off heat and keeping the eggs warm.

Maiasaura *mothers built their nests about one body length apart, so they would have room to look over their eggs and newborn babies.*

This model of a Maiasaura *nest was made after Dr. Horner's discoveries in Montana. The fossil nests found by the paleontologist held both eggs and hatchlings.*

Dinosaur Discoveries

Paleontologists (scientists who study prehistoric life) once thought that all dinosaurs were slow-moving and not too smart. Then an exciting discovery changed their minds.

In 1978 paleontologist Jack Horner found the remains of a 75-million-year-old dinosaur nursery in Montana. The fossils included full-grown dinosaurs and babies from fourteen inches to three feet long. The babies were still in their nests. Their teeth were worn down from eating. Dr. Horner concluded that the adult dinosaurs were devoted parents that fed and protected their young. He named the new dinosaur *Maiasaura*, or "good mother lizard." His discovery helped convince paleontologists that many dinosaurs were active and intelligent animals.

PARASAUROLOPHUS
(par-ah-sore-oh-LOH-fus)
When: Late Cretaceous,
75–70 million years ago
Where: Alaska and Alberta,
Canada
- Long tubelike crest
- May have gathered in colonies to make nests and raise young

These two Parasaurolophus *could be mothers taking a break from baby care. While they rest, they keep watch for predators that might try to snatch a helpless hatchling.*

Soon the nests are filled with small hungry hatchlings. The mothers work hard gathering food and bringing it back to their babies. Thanks to their good care, the young *Maiasaura* grow quickly. In a few months, they are ready to leave the nest and begin finding their own food. In time the young dinosaurs will join the big, noisy duckbill herd as it moves on to new feeding grounds.

TSINTAOSAURUS
(chin-dow-SORE-us)
When: Late Cretaceous,
75–65 million years ago
Where: China
- Long tubelike crest
- May have made loud bellowing noises through flaps of skin at base of crest

Tsintaosaurus *had a tall crest that looked something like a unicorn's horn. It was one of the last dinosaurs to walk the earth.*

This fossil skeleton of a Maiasaura *was found in Montana. Fossils help paleontologists figure out what dinosaurs looked like and how they lived.*

THE LAST DINOSAURS

Dinosaurs walked the earth for millions of years. Over time, different kinds appeared and died out. Duckbills were one of the last kinds of dinosaurs. Sixty-five million years ago, the duckbills and all the other remaining dinosaurs became extinct. Scientists have come up with many possible explanations, but no one knows for sure what killed the dinosaurs.

Today paleontologists continue to dig up and study fossils left behind by huge herds of *Maiasaura*. Their studies have already changed the way we think about dinosaurs. Who knows what mysteries of prehistoric life they will solve next?

Dinosaur Family Tree

ORDER

All dinosaurs are divided into two large groups, based on the shape and position of their hipbones. Ornithischians had backward-pointing hipbones.

SUBORDER

Ornithopods were two- or four-legged plant-eaters with birdlike feet, beaks, and stiff tails.

INFRAORDER

Hadrosaurs had bulky bodies, long flat beaks, and hundreds of grinding teeth.

FAMILY

A family includes one or more types of closely related dinosaurs.

GENUS

Every dinosaur has a two-word name. The first word tells us what genus, or type, of dinosaur it is. The genus plus the second word are its species—the group of very similar animals it belongs to. (For example, *Maiasaura peeblesorum* is one species of *Maiasaura*.)

Scientists organize all living things into groups, according to features shared.
This chart shows the groupings of the duck-billed plant-eaters described in this book.

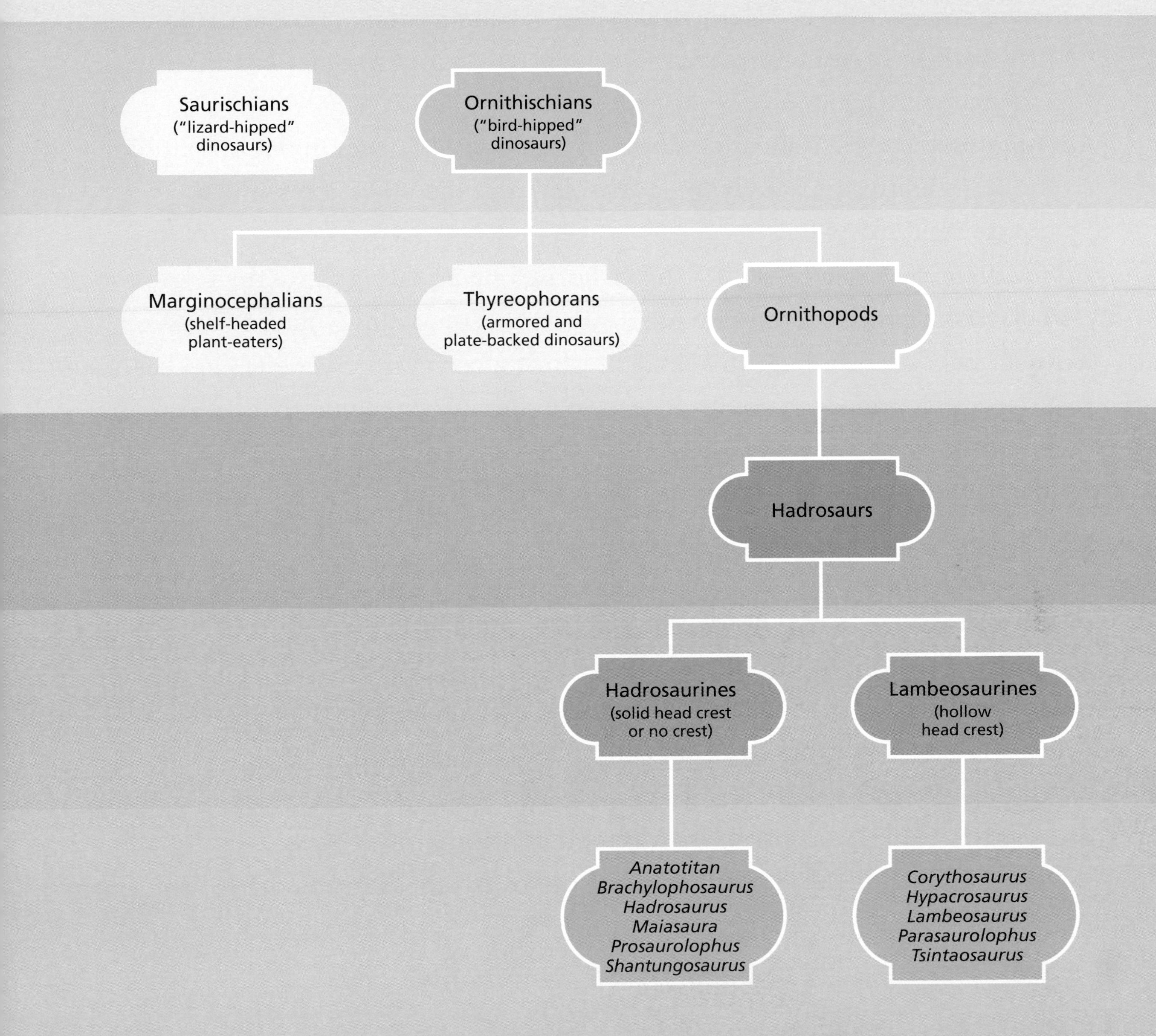

Glossary

***Albertosaurus*:** one of North America's most common tyrannosaurs (two-fingered meat-eating dinosaurs), which lived from about 80 million to 65 million years ago

Cretaceous (krih-TAY-shus) **period:** the time period from about 135 million to 65 million years ago, when *Maiasaura* and the other duck-billed dinosaurs lived

Einiosaurus (eye-nee-oh-SORE-us)**:** a horned plant-eating dinosaur related to *Triceratops*, which lived in North America in the Late Cretaceous period

extinct: no longer existing; an animal is extinct when every one of its kind has died

fossils: the hardened remains or traces of animals or plants that lived many thousands or millions of years ago

hadrosaurs: a group of plant-eating dinosaurs with bulky bodies, long flat beaks, and hundreds of cheek teeth, which were the most common land animals of the Late Cretaceous period; also called duck-billed dinosaurs or duckbills

mammals: animals that are warm-blooded, breathe air, and nurse their young with milk; humans are mammals

paleontologists (pay-lee-on-TAH-luh-jists)**:** scientists who study fossils to learn about dinosaurs and other forms of prehistoric life

predators: animals that hunt and kill other animals for food

pterosaurs (TEHR-uh-sores)**:** flying reptiles with wings almost forty feet across, which lived throughout most of the Age of Dinosaurs

Find Out More

Books

Cohen, Daniel. *Triceratops and Other Cretaceous Plant-Eaters.* Minneapolis: Capstone Press, 1996.

Holmes, Thom, and Laurie Holmes. *Peaceful Plant-Eating Dinosaurs.* Berkeley Heights, NJ: Enslow, 2001.

Horner, John R., and James Gorman. *Maia: A Dinosaur Grows Up.* Philadelphia: Running Press, 1987.

The Humongous Book of Dinosaurs. New York: Stewart, Tabori, and Chang, 1997.

Lindsay, William. *On the Trail of Incredible Dinosaurs.* New York: Dorling Kindersley, 1998.

Marshall, Chris, ed. *Dinosaurs of the World.* 11 vols. New York: Marshall Cavendish, 1999.

Parker, Steve. *The Age of the Dinosaurs.* Vol. 9, *The Hadrosaurs.* Danbury, CT: Grolier Educational, 2000.

Patent, Dorothy Hinshaw. *In Search of the Maiasaurs.* New York: Marshall Cavendish, 1999.

On-Line Sources*

***Dinosaur WebQuest* at**
http://schools.sbe.saskatoon.sk.ca/DE/1-4/2/dinowq.htm#chart
Designed by elementary school teachers in Saskatchewan, Canada, this site includes lots of information on many kinds of dinosaurs. Click on "Maiasaura" or another dinosaur name for an information sheet with basic facts and illustrations, including one you can print out to make a stand-up dinosaur model.

***Dinosphere* at http://tcm.childrensmuseum.org/dinosphere**
This site is based on the Dinosphere exhibit of Cretaceous period life at the Children's Museum of Indianapolis. Click on "Media Information" for a fact sheet on *Maiasaura*, or check out "Dinosaur Facts" for information and photos relating to dinosaur fossils.

***Introduction to Hadrosaurs, University of California, Berkeley, Museum of Paleontology* at**
http://www.ucmp.berkeley.edu/diapsids/ornithischia/hadrosauria.html
This article provides a good introduction to duck-billed dinosaurs plus photos of baby *Maiasaura* and other hadrosaur fossils.

***Zoom Dinosaurs* at http://www.zoomdinosaurs.com**
This colorful site from Enchanted Learning Software includes a world of information on dinosaur-related topics: dinosaur myths, records, behavior, and fossils; dinosaur fact sheets; quizzes, puzzles, printouts, and crafts; tips on writing a school report; and more.

**Website addresses sometimes change. For more on-line sources, check with the media specialist at your local library.*

Index

Virginia Schomp grew up in a quiet suburban town in northeastern New Jersey, where eight-ton duck-billed dinosaurs once roamed. In first grade she discovered that she loved books and writing, and in sixth grade she was named "class bookworm," because she always had her nose in a book. Today she is a freelance author who has written more than forty books for young readers on topics including careers, animals, ancient cultures, and modern history. Ms. Schomp lives in the Catskill Mountain region of New York with her husband, Richard, and their son, Chip.